His hand
my journey

3-3-21
Sandy,
Choose Joy!

☺ Joyce Barth

joyce barth

This book was printed in the United States of America.

ISBN: 978-1078291231

Formatting and cover design by Ryan Byrnes

Contents

Preface

The earliest pages of my journals were all chicken scratch with lots of tear stains. In later pages the words were stronger and more confident, and I realized I had a story to tell. This has been very therapeutic for me. I pray this book will somehow give you hope. Inspire you. Or touch your life in some way. I truly hope it blesses you just as it has been such a source of comfort and healing for me.

God has a plan for each of our lives. That is why we must always have faith and stay the course.

Joyce Barth

In the Beginning

I don't claim to be a religious guru by any stretch of the imagination, but there have been so many times in the past years I've seen His hand in my life and I find I must share. Take this for what it's worth and what you can use in your life, but His hand has truly been in my life and changed me in so many ways. It's with that I have decided to share my journey.

This book is about changing myself from the inside to the outside. It's not a quick fix, but a continual work in progress. This book is about giving hope and making small daily changes that can make an impact on your entire life just as they have mine.

Have you ever struggled with anything in your life? Finances, or perhaps your weight? Have you ever struggled with feeling like you weren't enough? Have you ever just wanted to do more, be more and have more? Well, that was me. Now don't get me wrong, I have a good life, good husband, amazing kids, career I loved, social

3

schedule that kept us hopping, and yet I was unhappy with me. How I looked. How I felt. More importantly, how I thought. I knew there were things missing and it was going to be up to me to make those changes. Little did I know the path I would have to walk in order to make some of these changes and how it was going to affect my entire life.

My parents were hard-working people. We were considered your typical middle-class family. Having grown up with farming in the family blood, hard work every day was the name of the game. My dad's motto was, "You have to work hard so you can play hard." My parents taught me to always have a smile on my face and a kind word for everyone I met. That positive attitude would take me far in life. I truly believe that is a critical key to your happiness. They also taught me about integrity, morals, values, and how important these are. Rules were enforced. What they said was respected. I didn't talk back (too much) because I knew that would get me into more trouble. However, being the youngest of four children, I also got by with more than my older siblings did for sure and of course I took full advantage.

I grew up with a strict Catholic background. We went to church every Saturday afternoon. We left the house 45 minutes early so we could get a close parking place, giving Dad time to take a nap before we went into church. With that being said, I did find it ironic my parent's home never contained a Bible.

When I was younger, we spent lots of time visiting our grandparents, relatives, and close friends of my parents. The parents would sit and visit or play Pinochle or Euchre and the kids would watch TV or play games. We were to be seen and not heard and were well-reminded of that when we went to visit. When you have 15 sets of aunts and uncles, there was always somewhere to go.

As I got a little older, my parents became very involved with an organization in Highland, IL by the name of Helvetia Sharpshooters. The group had a dance hall that was in severe need of renovation. My dad, along with a handful of other individuals, decided to make this into something more than a rundown dance hall. I spent many, many hours there throughout my childhood years and yes, the group did remodel it into something truly amazing to me.

I have so many fond memories of my childhood there. I made many great friends. I watched my parents give of their time and talents so freely and yet enjoying themselves to no end. Watching my parents volunteer made me realize how important it was to give back to a community you are proud of and love. My parents' love of giving back and volunteering their time was instilled in me. It has left an imprint on me to this day. This group turned the hall into a beautiful venue that housed many weddings and anniversary celebrations. The hall held dances every Saturday evening for years, up until just a few years ago. It is now solely used as a wedding venue.

His hand, my journey

The group of people that were involved since my dad's passing have maintained this hall and continue to beautify it. I honestly believe this is also where my love for music came from. As well as my love for bling on my attire. As I would sit as a child and watch the many beautiful women come in with their fancy sequin and blingy dresses, I would imagine myself as a grownup in those types of dresses.

For my dad, his true love was the flower beds out at the Lindendale Park. Every year, my dad would go to pick out every flower that was to be planted in every bed. He then went to work very tediously, I might add, measuring, and making sure every plant was put in precisely and in straight rows. He was very meticulous with these flowers and watered and took care of them with tender loving care. Heaven forbid if anyone messed with one of his flower beds. We all heard about it for days. They were so beautiful. I always loved walking through there knowing it was his pride and joy. As his health started to fail in his later years, his younger brother Tony took on the responsibility of helping him with those flowers. It made me smile and warmed my heart to see brothers in their later years working so well together.

Dad's meticulous nature continued at home with his well landscaped lawn. There was only one way to cut lawn and that was Fritz's way! When people came to visit, no one had better even think about putting a tire on his lawn or they would hear about it. If someone pulled in the driveway and "took their half out of the middle" as he referred to it, he made sure to let everyone know, especially my friends as we started driving. He may sound like he was a very strict man, which he was, but oh did he LOVE to have FUN. He and my mom did just that. They danced. They travelled. They fished and they loved their family. When those granddaughters came along, those girls could do no wrong in my parents eyes, especially my dad. The four granddaughters had him right where they wanted him. In addition, my dad owned the local sanitation business in Highland, IL for about 10 years or so. His motto was; your trash, is my cash. He was known for having the cleanest trash trucks in the area.

My mom, on the other hand, was quieter. I always remember her telling me dad was the one to bring her out of her shell. He told her she needed to talk and be social. Boy she did! When they decided to get involved with the Sharpshooters and the dance hall had been renovated, my mom started working with the local catering companies cooking for the wedding receptions at the Lindendale Ballroom. She grew to love cooking so much that she started her own catering business. She had her own set of ladies help her prepare and serve the food, including yours truly. Besides, I really didn't have a lot of choice, but it did get me out to see people. Again, being brought up around all of this helped me to become the person I am today. My love for being around people stems back from when I was younger.

When my dad bought his business, Mom became the bookkeeper. After my dad sold the business and she had retired from catering, she then went to work as a cook at a retirement facility. She really enjoyed it and continued to do so up until my dad passed. She then went back again after his passing, just to give her something to do. She continued to live life to the fullest. She enjoyed many card games, bingo games, gambling trips, even taking a trip to Europe one time.

I had the typical childhood for the most part. To earn extra cash, I babysat, helped my mom with her catering business and held part time jobs. I graduated from high school and immediately went to work in St. Louis, MO for what was to be my forever career. In the 1980's, the goal was to find a great company to work for and stay there long term. I went through a couple of job changes, but really thought I had found my place in the insurance industry. However, traveling back and forth every day to the city got the best of me. After 11 years of commuting, I decided I needed to find an opportunity closer to home. I was married at that point and was starting a new chapter in life. For these reasons, I went to work locally and also started a part-time career in direct sales. Additional stress and just day to day things started to get the best of me. The marriage started to suffer.

I decided to quit my corporate job to pursue my direct sales opportunity since I had found some success. I think it was at this point I noticed my first "aha" as I shall call it, or the first time I noticed God's hand in my life. I wasn't quite sure why I was quitting my job at that exact point in time, but I followed what I felt led to do. Six weeks after I quit, my parents were on vacation and my dad became extremely ill. I needed to fly to where they were to be with them. These were to be the final weeks of my dad's life. I was able to be there for my family and spend all those last days with my dad. In the process, the loss of my father gave me even more sadness. Enter an unhappy person. Oh I kept my game face on for quite some time, but it came to the point, where I just could not continue on in my marriage.

Thus, resulting in a divorce. Something of which I never thought would be me.

I found myself single again. I was having great success in my direct sales business. I also knew I wasn't cut out to be a single person on my own. I loved having people around. My personality is to have fun and be around people that bring happiness and joy. So to find myself being alone, was a hard pill for me to swallow.

As I continued on, I just knew there were things missing. However, I could not quite put my finger on what all those missing pieces were. Looking back now, God definitely had his hand on my life and how it was to play out. However, I didn't even remotely see that at the time.

Life With Augie

I knew I longed to be married and have a family. So when Augie entered my life, it was totally by accident. This would be the second time I noticed God's hand in my life. I had gone to work at a local pub just to be around people. It was by chance Aug and his daughter Amanda came in for a pizza and soda one summer Saturday afternoon. It sparked conversation and six weeks later, we had our first date.

I had known Aug for some years through my older sister; however, I hadn't seen him in quite some time. When our paths connected, little did I know I would become an instant mother of four. I often joked I went from being single with no kids, to being married with four kids, all within a matter of minutes, but I truly feel God knew I needed and wanted a family. Plus, Aug and the kids really needed a female figure in their lives.

As we started our life together, there were of course the normal ups and downs and definitely lots of changes for all of us while we tried to find a happy medium for a blended family. Along with this came a name change for me. Oh yes, my last name changed, but my first name also changed. I went from being called Joyce to now being called Joycie! I embraced that and still am called that to this day. That's what the kids and Aug chose to call me and boy has it stuck. Things were going along pretty well despite the normal bumps in the road that come along with marriage and parenting. However, with this also came additional stress and financial obligations which were totally different than what I was used to as a single person.

My career in direct sales was still going great. Having this career in my life taught me so many things and great skills I needed in my life overall. It taught me to be a better wife, a better mom and a better friend. It also taught me so many daily life skills as far as organization, disciplining my time, but it ultimately taught me about how important faith was. It was the faith, family, career philosophy which I whole heartedly embraced.

Life with Aug was interesting to say the least! He was a lifelong farmer in St. Rose, IL. When he sold his farm, he always said, "Once a farmer, always a farmer." It was something in your blood. He would help his good friend Paul on his farm every opportunity he had. Aug always commented how he loved the smell of the earth when it was planting or harvest time. After we got together, I moved to St. Rose. I immediately felt like I was at home. This community is a very tight-knit community where everyone looks out for each other and helps each other out in a time of need. It's a predominantly Catholic community. Going to church on Saturday or Sunday was the thing to do. It is also a community of people who like to have fun and enjoy themselves. Work hard so you can play hard! They followed my dad's motto, so I knew I would fit in. In fact, I can remember when I was younger my dad always told me I needed to move to St. Rose so he could come there to visit me since he loved the community. I'm sure he is smiling down on me for sure.

There was never a dull moment around our house. With two kids living with us full time who were both very social and active and the other two here for holidays and summers, it was non-stop action. Aug drove a truck for a living. In the spring and fall, there were many long hours for sure. He didn't mind though. He would get up early (usually around 3:00 am) and take off for the day. One of his mottos was, "You gotta get started so you can get finished."

The kids were in sports, so there were events to attend. We also held a very tight social schedule. Whether it was attending a wedding or a fundraiser or going to a friend's home to sit back and catch up, we were always on the go.

Aug also insisted on always having a project going on around the house. He was constantly looking for ways to improve things that needed to be built or done. It was just who he was. I can remember when we decided to do a house

16

remodel. He decided we needed to extend the garage. We got a call from the contractor on a Saturday morning, letting us know they would be here on Monday to start the construction of the garage. There was only one problem with the two-day notice; Aug had told them he would have the old wall torn down and everything would be ready for them to go when they wanted to start. Now mind you, this is on a Saturday morning, and he was working. I called him frantically, telling him what the contactor had just told me. He said, "Joycie, not to worry. I have it under control. I will make sure everything is ready to go on Monday when they get there. Your only job is to make sure we have plenty of food and beer for the people who are going to be helping us." I said, "Oh, you have that all lined up already?" He said, "No, but don't you worry. By 1:00 pm this afternoon there will be a crew there and we will get it taken care of."

Guess what, he wasn't lying! By that afternoon, we had a crew, equipment, and they all went to work taking the wall down and getting it prepped and ready to go for Monday morning. I was so touched and impressed by this. Aug always shared with me how the people of St. Rose helped each other out when needed. It definitely came to action that day as I witnessed what all transpired in a matter of hours.

The tradition of helping each other out is so strong here in St. Rose, IL. Many of the surrounding communities always comment on how unique and impressive it is the way we stand and pull together. Makes me very, very proud to be part of St. Rose.

As this remodel continued, I had to go out of town for a few days. On the day I was due to return, Aug gave me a phone call on my way home and said, "Joycie, don't be alarmed, but when you get home, you may have a hard time getting into the house. We tore off all the steps to get in, and the new ones haven't been poured as of yet." Well, I thought he was joking. But low and behold, when I got home that evening after a 15-hour drive, in the rain for the last two hours, all I wanted to do was to walk in to my house and lay down to sleep. It was a challenge to even get in the house to say the least. He wasn't lying.

When I pulled up, the front porch was totally gone! The steps from the garage into the house were also gone. I'm like, holy crap, how am I going to get in the house with my luggage? I'm vertically challenged to say the least, and I'm not a sprinter who can run and jump in. So, let me just give you a visual of getting in the house. Heft my luggage up. Throw it into the house. Jump up to sit my butt down on the door entry. Swing my legs around to get into the house. Can you imagine? Not a happy camper, but a funny memory for sure. Needless to say, the next day we had some makeshift steps for me to get in and out of the house. The remodel did turn out amazing and I absolutely love everything about it.

Another one of Aug's projects was the construction of a pavilion in our back yard. He thought it would be a great addition for us, so we could have people over and also a place to house all of his stuff. Aug was a collector of stuff. You never knew when you might need this stuff, so we never threw anything away, ever! He was telling me about this pavilion he was going to build and gave me the dimensions. I am a rather visual person. I had no clue how big this thing was going to be. While I was out of town (yes there is a pattern here), I returned to find this ginormous pavilion going up in our back yard. I am like, "What on earth are you building?" Aug said, "Joycie I told you before you left, I was going to start building the pavilion." I said, "Yes I know but I had no idea it was going to be this big!" He said, "I know that's why I figured I would just go ahead and have it under construction when you returned because, that way you could see how big it was going to be." I literally had to laugh out loud because he knew I would probably pitch a fit had I been around. However, it was already done. What was I going to do? Besides that, I was the one who said I was a visual person, so better be careful what I say.

Once we purchased our jeep, which was bright yellow, we spent a lot of hours on the road jeeping. Never off-roading it, but just putz-ing

down the country roads checking crops or
enjoying the scenery. We spent a lot of good
times in the jeep with the kids or family and
friends. Those were precious memories I hold
dear to this day. That jeep still remains my
summer toy.

Projects were Aug's middle name. He bought
an old truck one time and decided he wanted to
paint it yellow, since we had purchased a yellow
jeep. In his mind all his vehicles should be yellow.
So he went to work. Taking the truck apart.
Prepping it. Getting it ready for painting.

It was quite a long project. Sandblasting and
doing whatever needed to be done to prepare it.
It turned into a family project. He and the girls
had so much fun doing this together. Priceless
memories for everyone. We still have some
remnants of paint left on the pavilion floor too.

Once the truck was done, he decided he
wanted to take an old truck trailer and paint it
yellow as well. I was like, "What are you going to
do with that trailer?" His response, "Joycie, I am

21

gonna hook it up to the jeep and we are going to travel around the country for a Sunday Funday putz-ing around day with the kids or with friends." Hence that is how it all came about. Sure enough that is exactly what we did! The trailer was loaded with lawn chairs. He even went so far as to try and mount seats in it one time. The man had an imagination. He was willing to try anything just one time. As you can tell, there was always something going on and fun was going to be had if Augie was involved.

We had "Quiet Mondays" where there was supposed to be no talking because he always said I was going to run out of words. Ha, that never happened. He occasionally had what he also called "No Pants Day," and yep, you guessed it. He said, "My house, my prerogative." Gotta love it! Sunday nights were always school nights, so we had to get home early. You can ask any of our family or friends about these special days. They will all laugh and vouch on how true all of this was. Welcome to the world of Augie!

We were always involved with the St. Rose Development Club. We worked on whatever functions they had to raise money for the community. Aug held various offices throughout the years. When I moved in to town, it was just a given I would also get involved. Having watched my parents all those years volunteering, I just jumped in to do what I could as well.

At one point, Aug volunteered me to take over chairing the Lenten Fish Fry's at the park. He said I would be great at it and he would help however he could. He thought I would be the perfect chairperson for the event, given it was originally an idea I had when I moved to St. Rose. Not to mention I have amazing organizational skills. That was a huge undertaking, but I am so glad I did it. It turned out to be a lot of fun for everyone. I chaired that event for five years and then turned it over to our daughter Megan. Who is still co-chairing it to this day.

Aug's passion for philanthropy grew even more when he decided to become a Mason and a Ma-Cli-Bo Shriner. He had always been a huge history buff and the mystery of the Masons intrigued him. I remember one day when we went to visit the local Masonic Temple. He and the gentleman showing him around spent a couple hours talking about all of the rich history. Once he completed his Masonry work, he went on to be a Shriner since that was his passion. My brother Dave and a good friend of his, Mark, as well as a couple of other local Shriners were instrumental in getting Aug involved. Once he did, he was a lifer and marched in countless parades. Our summer weekends then became which parade were we going to this weekend. The Ma-Cli-Bo Shriners became like a family to us. We spent so many weekends together. I still remain close with them all to this day. Aug was everyone's favorite friendly gorilla and later, the waving chipmunk with his distinct wave.

There was never a dull moment with Augie. These are just a few of the great memories of him! I could go on and on.

Challenges = Strength

While life with Aug was good for the most part, there were also times that weren't always so great and proved to be challenging in our marriage. As I said, when we first got married, financial obligations were bothering me, and I was having a hard time dealing with it. Aug was a super hard worker. However, our views on finances were different. I was the worrier, and his motto was "get up every day and make more."

We were the typical family that had more month than money. There is a verse in the Bible that says, "And my God will meet all your needs according to the riches of his glory in Christ Jesus" (Philippians 4:19 NIV). At that time, I hadn't found that verse, so I was continually circling the same mountain trying to figure it out.

We are given tests throughout our lives. We have to pass those tests before we can be given more. During that time, God spoke to me that we needed to get our finances in order. We had not been very good stewards of what He had given us. There is a saying that until you submit to what He has in store and totally give it to Him, you will continue to fight the same battles. "'Bring the whole tithe into the storehouse, that there may be food in my house. Test me in this,' says the LORD Almighty, 'and see if I will not throw open the floodgates of heaven and pour out so much blessing that there will not be room enough to store it.'" (Malachi 3:10 NIV). So in that instant, I vowed we would be better stewards and praise him and I vowed that I would drop money in the collection basket every Sunday.

Of course, I shared this with Augie. At first he looked at me like I had three heads. However, over time, he began to see what I saw. It was simply amazing. It didn't happen overnight by any means. But in time, our faithfulness and continued tithing gave way to some huge changes for us. Augie believed in it so much, he started to tell his trucking buddies about it. I always thought I knew better but once we let Him take the reign, it has been amazing. He continues to guide me to this day on my financial journey.

Augie and I had hit a major speed bump in our marriage that I wasn't expecting. It honestly took a toll on me, physically and emotionally. I had always been a pretty happy-go-lucky type gal, so this was a very tough time for me. This made me start to second guess myself. My self-esteem took a huge hit. I turned to food for solace. I ate when I was sad. I ate when I was nervous. I ate when I was bored. Of course, I always tried to keep a smile on my face; however, there were times that I just couldn't hardly bear it. I was mad. I was sad. I was hurt. I think I felt every emotion a person could possibly feel in those days, which turned into months. I started to pack on the pounds.

Looking back today at photos, I had no idea of how much weight I had put on. I was very thankful for family and friends who were there for me during this period. There were people who prayed with me. Cried with me. They were there with a shoulder for me to lean on during all of this. I chose to lean on God, believe and have faith that we would get through the speed bump. "I can do all this through him who gives me strength" (Philippians 4:13 NIV). Although nothing had really changed in our situation, everything changed in the instant I chose once again to have faith and listen to His words rather than trying to control the situation myself.

Food became everything to me. It was comfort. It was a de-stressor. It was a treat. It was pretty much what I focused on all the time. Now, I have never been skinny. My doctor told me many years ago I would never be skinny because of my family make-up and genetics. However, he told me I could be much healthier than I was. I had always struggled with my weight. I was using every excuse in the book, but bottom line there really wasn't any excuse, except that I was making poor choices.

In 2012, I had hit my all-time high in weight and I was miserable. Once again, I felt my confidence level sinking even more and not feeling great about myself. Not to mention the extra weight was taking a toll on my body. I needed to get this figured out because I wasn't getting any younger. I didn't want my health to suffer.

I had been taught many years ago that positive affirmations were critical and positive self-talk was a must. I had success with this in areas of my business. At the urging of one of my mentors, I decided I would start affirming things in my personal life. One of those affirmations was to get my weight in order.

I went through all of 2012 affirming my weight loss. However, my weight issue still weighed heavily on me. I had tried everything from tracking calories to journaling how I felt about what I was eating and when. After about a week of that, I nixed that idea. I decided I would do the best I could do and try to make better choices, knowing it was a process. At the end of that year, I had lost a whopping eight pounds. Nothing to write home about. However, I hadn't gained anything. I felt it was a start.

Joyce Barth

The beginning of 2013, I had the opportunity to spend a few days with my sister in Florida. Those times on the beach or sitting out by the palm trees have always been so inspirational and eye opening to me. In my alone time, I realized my prayer life and quiet time had gone stagnant. I wasn't growing spiritually. God had a plan. He always does. When the student is ready, the teacher appears as they say. I made a vow to God I would get myself back in great spiritual shape, so I could be the best I could be. To be a blessing to others in order to glorify Him.

I was able to connect with a couple of spiritual mentors, and I felt a year of growth in that area of my life. It was absolutely huge. What I was learning from all of this was first, I had to go to Him with everything in every area of my life. "But seek first his kingdom and his righteousness, and all these things will be given to you as well" (Matthew 6:33 NIV). When I would submit to Him and discipline myself, great things would happen and He would be able to bless me.

Aug and I were also working on a house addition that year. We had come up with the perfect plan and thought we had everything in place. However, we hit obstacle after obstacle, road block after road block. I prayed that everything would work out to our advantage. After months and months of trying to make this come to fruition, Aug and I decided together, we would just wait and work on that project at a later time. Looking back now, I once again realize God's hand was in all of this. The addition would have been way more space than I would need in the future. Plus the financial burden would have been great on me. I took that as a sign that God was in control of the situation, even though at the time this was all happening, I had no idea why every path was being blocked.

In this same year, I vowed to get more disciplined with business and continue on my weight loss journey as well. Needless to say, 2013 was a year of growth. First in my spiritual walk, but also my marriage grew stronger than before. My business grew and had success. I was still working on healthy eating lifestyle changes and lost another whopping eight pounds over the course of a year.

While I have to admit I felt a little defeated, there were a few things God shed light on to me. First of all, I didn't put all of that weight on overnight, it wasn't going to come off overnight. Second of all, it takes daily discipline, not once in a while discipline. While I knew tracking every morsel was not going to work for me, I had to find something that would work for me.

During 2013, I grew in my spiritual walk. A very good friend of mine had started on a healthy eating plan and shared some of her tips with me. While I had watched and admired many of my friends losing weight and getting healthy bodies, when I would ask them their secrets or success tips, many seemed too restrictive to me, so I immediately dismissed it. However, this friend kept it very simple. She shared some things she was eating and what she wasn't eating. It seemed maybe something I could give a try. I watched her body transform. Yet, she was still enjoying herself. Her diet didn't really seem as though it had disrupted her lifestyle at all. Maybe I could try this and see if it would work.

I am a huge pasta fan. I always joked with Aug that if I ate a plate of spaghetti, you may as well tape it to my butt because that was where it was going to end up. At the very end of 2013, on Christmas Eve to be exact, I received a call from my doctor. My blood work had come back. Since I was getting older, my triglycerides and cholesterol needed to get in check, and I need to start working on that immediately. Can you imagine, getting a call like that right before Christmas? Seriously! What was that doctor thinking? Like I am really going to eat healthy during the holidays. I decided I would tackle that as a New Year's goal.

I had just become a first-time grandma. I was getting my affirmations in place once again for 2014. A mantra came to me, "Fit and Fabulous at 50" because I was turning 50 in July of 2014. I just happened to sit down and watched a portion of an episode of the Dr. Oz show one day at lunch. I saw an interview with Tory Johnson on the show. She was a Good Morning America contributor. She was on the show telling about a book she had written called *The Shift: How I Finally Lost Weight and Discovered a Happier Life.* I'm like, "Hm, maybe I should order that book." After all, I had never watched the Dr. Oz show.

I was working on my affirmations again and this was put in front of me; perhaps I should be listening. Was this God speaking to me? When the student is ready, the teacher appears. I ordered this book. The day the book arrived, it was snowing so bad I couldn't see the road. Reading is something I didn't enjoy. However, this book spoke to me. I read it in a day and a half. It really helped me immensely. This book taught me a lot. It really helped me to make a shift in my thinking as far as my weight went. I truly believe God had been working on these things with me for a long time and continues to work on so many areas in my life. I am so thankful I'm working to be a better student. I'm also thankful to the people he put in my life who were also making those healthy eating changes as I watched their transformation in front of my eyes. It made me want to join in that success.

The year 2014 was another year of changes for me. I'm proud to say I continued to grow in my spiritual walk, which was most important in my opinion. I continued to grow in a lot of areas in my life, learning new disciplines as well as making changes to my lifestyle.

Through my studies, I realized my body is a temple of God. I have to be good to that temple and treat it with high honor. Thus another reason, I wanted to make the commitment to being healthier so I can go out and bless others and glorify God. It wasn't about being skinny, but about being healthier than I have ever been. I have a lot of living to do yet and a lot of lives to change, so I intend on sticking around for a while and with God's help, I can do all of this.

Now as my for my mantra, Fit and Fabulous at 50. It was a great accomplishment I had that year. Weight loss for the entire year was 39 1/2 pounds, yippee! Giving me a three-year grand total of 55 1/2 pounds. It has been a journey of lifestyle changes for me. I know without a doubt it has been a prayerful and affirmative time. I am so thankful God has shown me the way. I have an extra bounce in my step and more energy. While I felt I was still a work in progress in all areas of my life, my doctor called me on the day before Christmas Eve that year, she had these words to say: "All of your counts are excellent." She was super happy with the changes I had made, but what made her the happiest was that I did it the good, old fashioned, natural way. Watching portions, exercising (sometimes), eating healthier foods, and making better choices.

Blessed to be a Blessing

As I have been so blessed with a great career in my direct sales business, it gave me opportunities to bless my amazing mother. My mom was always very active. However, at the age of 79 she started to finally slow down a bit. That's when my sister and I decided we were going to start taking Mom on girls trips, to have the experience and memories with her. The memories we made and pictures we took will last a lifetime. We went to a lot of fun places like Myrtle Beach, SC; Lake of the Ozarks, MO; Virginia Beach, VA; Charleston, SC. These were all great trips. However, when asking my mom what her favorite trips were, she said for sure New York City and California.

We decided to celebrate her 80th birthday where my sister and I treated Mom to an all-expense-paid trip to New York City at Christmas time. We did everything first class. It was a trip of a lifetime that my mother always remembered and talked about until the day she died. We stayed in Times Square, saw The Rockettes, and saw the Macy's Window display. We drove through Central Park, went to a Broadway show and had 6th row seats, shopped in SoHo, saw the sights around the Twin Towers. We visited the famous Christmas Tree in Rockefeller Center, the Brooklyn Bridge, and all of the lights and displays on 7th Avenue. So many amazing memories were made on that trip.

I have to tell you about one person we crossed paths with on this trip. I know without a doubt God placed him in my path a few years earlier on a previous trip to New York City. Big Mo was my chauffeur on a previous trip. When we decided to take my mom to New York, we knew because of her age we were going to need someone to help take extra special care of her needs. We wanted to treat her like royalty. So I contacted Big Mo. He was more than happy to attend to my mom's every need.

What we found out on this trip was Big Mo was a very devoted Christian. I honestly believe God wanted our paths to cross once again. I believe this because he and I remain in contact and remain friends. There have been times over the years, when he would just send a quick note to say Hi, ask for prayers and vice versa. When he learned of my mother's passing, he sent the sweetest note and prayer. It still amazes me how God has our paths cross with certain people who will forever remain etched in our lives.

2014 would be the last year my sister and I took my mom on an annual girl's trip. As my mom's health started to fail, we decided this would be the last trip we would be able to take her on. We wanted to make it a bucket list trip for her. She wanted to go to California to visit a good friend of mine by the name of Kelly. Kelly had been a family friend for years. When she lived in St. Louis, she spent numerous weekends with my family. So of course, my mom wanted to go see her since it had been years.

Mom watched practically every Price is Right episode after she retired. We decided we were going to get tickets to the show for her. So on the morning of the show, we got in the car and headed down the California Freeway to attend a taping. We were met with every obstacle possible that day.

First off, we had done a trial run to our exit on a previous day. When we set out, we allowed ourselves an additional 45 minutes due to unexpected volumes of traffic. That didn't work out very well at all because we were stuck in a traffic jam like no other! Here we were sitting on the freeway and we were supposed to be at the show in 30 minutes. Needless to say, I started praying feverishly, because I so wanted this for my mom.

When we finally got to our exit, low and behold, the darn thing was closed for construction that day. Are you kidding me? Ok, we've got this, on to the next exit. I'm praying as my sister is feverishly re-routing her GPS. We take the exit we were given and were headed to the parking area shown. We had only five minutes to spare. We pull into the parking lot only to be told we were in the wrong parking lot. We had to go around the corner to the next lot.

We were also told we needed to be there twenty minutes ago to get in to the lot and to the taping. At this point, I was like, "Okay Lord, if we are supposed to be at this taping, you are going to have to do some serious work here." So as not to give up, I vamoosed around the corner. I pulled into the lot and met the sweetest gal. I told her our story and she immediately found us a spot to park. She radioed ahead that we were on our way. She assured us we would still be able to get in to the taping. Woohoo, prayers answered.

Oh no, it gets better! As we arrived into the taping area, we found out we were the final three guests. We had arrived in just the nick of time. Now if you've ever been to the Price is Right, every person goes through an interview process. We went through the interview process. They were asking all of us questions about our favorite game and where we were from.

My mom professed her love for the show and how she watched it every day. When it came to me, well not so much, as I never watch the show. Giggle, giggle. As they walked away from us, my sister jokingly said to me, "I think you are going to be called as a contestant, because when they were talking to you, the assistant was writing things down." I laughed and said, "Oh whatever." As we get into the stage area and seated, I jokingly said to my sister, "Better get my lip gloss on so I'm camera ready." We had so much fun watching the taping. To watch my mother's face was a memory I will never forget. She was just in awe of everything. It was such a blessing to me.

But oh yes, we aren't done just yet. Last contestant's name was ready to be called. "Joyce Barth, come on down, you are the next contestant on the Price is Right!" I looked at my sister and I looked at my mom and I'm like oh crap, that's me!

I started screaming, and headed down to contestants row. My prize came out on stage to bid on and low and behold I was the closest to the actual price. Up on stage I go, meeting the Drew Carey. Well I would like to tell you I won big at my game, but not so much. However, I did redeem myself. When I spun the wheel, I actually won a spot on the Showcase. Did I win my showcase? Nope, sure didn't, but that's ok. The memories made that day were all I needed.

The most priceless thing for me was seeing my mom's beaming face when I met her after the show. Her smile and her eyes were glistening with happy tears. When I walked up to her she gave me a big hug and kiss and said, "Joyce Ann I am so proud of you," that was all I needed. I still thank God to this day for making that all happen and working everything out for us. Major God wink.

Joyce Barth

Something is Seriously Wrong

As we headed into 2015, there was a lot of excitement happening in our family. Two of our children were planning weddings for 2016. We were expecting and excited to meet our second grandbaby. Aug and I had started a new business venture purchasing the local car wash in town. My direct sales business was continuing to thrive. We were excited. Things were really coming together for us. It seemed as though we were on track in a lot of areas in our lives. Then Father's Day came. This was the day everything started to spiral in a downward motion for Aug.

Aug woke up that day and was not feeling well at all. We went to lunch with one of the children, and he felt so badly he couldn't eat at all which was totally unlike him. Figuring it was a flu bug, he brushed it off and didn't think too much about it. But as the week went on, he felt worse and worse. By the weekend, he decided he better get to a doctor to see what was going on. That was the start of many, many doctor visits, which led to many, many blood draws, which led to many, many other tests, which led to specialist after specialist to try and figure out what the mysterious illness was that Aug had or what was going on with his body.

He was losing weight. He was having horrible night sweats. He had no energy. He was having extreme pain in his back and basically felt like crap as he put it. There were times where he could hardly walk. He went from being the energetic and constantly on-the-go life of the party to a person who used all his energy to get through a day. I was watching him deteriorate before my very eyes.

I am a get-it-fixed-and-done sort of person. I started doing research online because if the doctors could not figure it out, I would. I started praying immediately for God to give us answers and lead us in the right direction so he could be better for the birth of his second grandchild which was quickly approaching. Thankfully, when Maverick August Barth (Aug's namesake was born), he felt great, which was an answer to a prayer.

However, his health continued to deteriorate and decline. His weight loss was continuing so much he was withering away to nothing. He was weak. He slept a lot. He forced himself to work because he was a trooper, but our lives had changed dramatically. I continued to pray but was frustrated. We were not getting any answers. The answers the doctors did give us did not line up with all of his symptoms. We spent so much time at doctor appointments, having tests and getting blood work done, yet we had not gotten to the true root of his health issue.

By the time the holidays rolled around, it took all he had to muster the energy to spend time with the family which was not him at all. I spent lots of time in prayer asking God for answers. As a side note, with all of this going on I was continuing on my healthy eating journey and thanked God for helping me with this because I was glad for the extra energy needed. I often wondered why after all the times I had tried to lose weight, why was it I was able to have success. I honestly felt like God had spoken to me; that all would be revealed in due time.

Happy New Year! 2016 was to be a magical year for our family. Our son was getting married to the girl of his dreams in June. Our daughter was to get married to the man of her dreams in July. Now, we just needed to get Aug feeling better. My patience was wearing thin. He was just exhausted. Together we were continuing on. We were determined to get answers to his mystery illness.

The morning of January 11th, Aug had multiple doctor appointments and blood work done. It seemed as though everything was in order. We left those appointments and were awaiting a follow up appointment with an oncologist later that week with the hope of getting some answers. We returned home and Aug decided to go to work for a couple of hours that afternoon. I was scheduled to leave town that week for a conference, so I was going to run some errands. I said I would meet him back at the house later in the afternoon.

I was on the road when I received a dreaded call from his place of employment. Something was severely wrong with Aug. He had lost all feeling in his right side and was having difficulty talking. They immediately called 911. I frantically returned to his work. By the time I arrived, EMS had him loaded up and told me they thought he had a stroke. EMS wanted to by-pass the small town hospital and take him directly to St. Louis to a hospital better equipped to handle this sort of thing. I gave the ok. I went to speak with Aug and said I would meet him at the hospital. Well you can imagine everything running through my head at that point? We had just left the doctor's office a few hours earlier. They told us everything was in order. How on earth could this be happening to him?

My daughter Megan and I headed to the hospital and contacted the other children to let them know what was happening. I immediately started to pray. Maybe now we would get the answers we need to heal this very ill man. The next hours and days were a series of ups and downs for him and for the family. The doctor's main question was why he would have had such a serious stroke when having absolutely no risk factors for a stroke. Of course, more testing needed to be done. Everyone was baffled.

After a couple days of more testing, we were met with a very solemn doctor who uttered these words to me and my daughter Kayla, "Your husband is a very sick man. He has a severe infection in the lining of his heart and is in very, very critical condition." Kayla and I looked at each other, dumbfounded, but almost relieved that at least now we had some answers. The doctor then went on to tell us the extent of the damage. We realized this was life-threatening. I can't even begin to tell you everything going through my mind at that moment. I was so glad Kayla was with me, because I know my mind immediately shut down. She was there to listen and hear everything the doctor had to say. We were told that two of his valves were not working at all and a third valve had severe damage. Open heart surgery was needed. However, because of the stroke and his weakness from the decline in health over the previous six months, his body was not strong enough to withstand surgery.

The next days were a vicious circle for him in and out of ICU, his heart going in and out of rhythm, trying to find an antibiotic strong enough to clear the infection around his heart without shutting down his other organs and doing more harm to him. I cannot tell you how many teams of physicians we saw at the hospital. I think we saw every team St. Louis University Hospital had on staff. As a family, we were trying to wrap our brain around all of this. We knew he had a long road ahead of him. However, we also knew he was strong and was a fighter. So we, along with hundreds of family and friends, started fervently praying for his strength to recover.

The day before Aug turned 59, we were in his ICU room playing a game of Euchre when the doctors came in and explained what the next steps of action would be in his recovery process.

Having suffered from expressive aphaysia from the stroke, his speech was almost impossible. However, the one thing he asked the doctor when he told him he was going to need to go to rehab before surgery was, "Why wait?" The doctor explained everything. I believe at this point, he realized how severe everything was.

In those next days it seemed as though Aug had started giving up hope. However, we as a family DID NOT. We continued to cheer him on. We fervently prayed, knowing he was going to be a walking miracle! I was standing on and believing in a miracle. Anyone that came into my space needed to believe that too. It was decided Aug was going to rehab to strengthen his body before surgery. Even though Aug could not speak, his blue eyes sure did a lot of talking when we told him that. He was not a fan at all! We assured him this would be the best thing. He needed to trust us and the doctors to make the best possible decisions at this point.

The night before he was due to be moved to a facility, he once again took a severe turn for the

worse. I had decided I would go home that
evening to try and get a little rest. The hospital
called me and told me his heart was very out of
rhythm. They suggested I come to the hospital. I
was on my way when I got the call he had gone
into cardiac arrest, but they had brought him
back. I had just walked into his ICU room to see
him and he once again went into cardiac arrest.
Once again, they were able to bring him back.
However, at this point, the doctors decided they
needed to put him on life support. His little body
needed some help to fight. I signed the papers to
put him on the machines.

At this point, the children had arrived, and we
were told the next hours and days were going to
be a touch-and-go situation. We were not given a
lot of assurance Aug was going to win this fight.
We reluctantly called his siblings to let them
know. It was an around the clock vigil with all of
us being together and watching Aug fight for his
life. Family and friends gathered with us to be a
source of comfort and support. The doctors did
not paint a rosy picture. We as a family were

going to have to make some hard decisions. This is not a conversation I wish on anyone in their lifetime!

Aug continued to fight. Even the doctors were amazed at one point. However, after 72+ hours of fighting, his little body could not fight any more. Aug Barth lost his battle around 9 am on Monday February 1, 2016. His body had become septic. Because of the infection in the lining of his heart, plus the stroke, everything shut down.

I share all of these details with you because through all of this, I never lost my faith in God. I prayed and believed without a shadow of a doubt knowing and believing Aug was going to be my walking miracle. However, in those last hours when the doctors told me it did not look good, my prayer changed to, "God your will be done." As hard as it was going to be if we lost him, it surely would not be fair to Aug to live a life less than what he was used to. Realistically no one was sure what his quality of life would have been.

The First Days After

So there I was, a widow at the age of 51, planning a funeral for my husband who passed away at far too young an age. I was trying to be strong for the children who had just lost their dad. Everyone was trying to wrap their minds around it. Those first few days were filled with numerous family members and friends stopping by the house to console us and to do whatever they could. However, we were numb. I was in a fog, to say the least.

I continued to pray the Lord would give me the strength to get through the visitation and the funeral without totally falling apart at the seams. I remember (well kind of) the hundreds of people who came by to pay their respects to the family. It was heart wrenching, but also so very touching to know how many people loved us and him.

The day he was laid to rest was a warm and sunny day for February. There were hundreds in attendance. As we travelled to his final resting place, it was done in a very unique style. The St.

Rose Fire Department was the honor guard as we entered the cemetery. Aug's casket was taken via the Ma-Cli-Bo Shriner motorhome with his casket in the motorhome cage and his Shriner buddies as the honorary guards. This was so fitting since he loved being a Shriner.

The children and I stuck together and were there for each other. We became #barthstrong.

I knew getting through this as a family was not going to be easy, but I had made a promise to Aug all those years ago that I would take care of the kids should something happen to him. That I must and will do. I refused to shrink back and become a feel-sorry-for-myself sort of person. Now don't get me wrong, there were many days where I would just sit and cry and cry and cry. I think I should have bought stock in Puffs or Kleenex. However, I also knew Aug had a motto he shared with me which was, "No matter what is going on in life, you have to get up every day and milk the cows." That became our family motto. On the days when we really didn't feel like it, we remembered that motto. This gave the children and I the strength of character to carry on.

My mother, Jean, had been a widow for 20 years. I watched her strength as she continued to truly live life after my father passed. So with the kids, my mom, our families, and our friends by our sides, we started a new normal of trying to regain some sort of order in our lives.

In those first days after Aug's passing, I struggled with immense guilt. Somehow I felt I had let him down. I realized very soon that was just Satan trying to torment me. I wrote a lot of letters to Aug. It helped ease the pain of loss I was feeling. Then there were times I was angry. Angry at Aug for leaving me. Angry at God for not saving Aug. Those were human feelings and I just had to deal with them.

Day by day, I would do the best I could to get myself up and get myself going. Those first weeks were filled with so many emotions. I never knew one person could cry so much, but I was grieving. I knew I needed to feel every ounce of that grief if I was ever to start the healing process. I was so thankful for my faith, because that was what would get me through the day.

As the days went on, I started to gain some strength. I would have my usual morning cry, as I sat in my prayer chair. I would ask God for enough strength just to get me through that day. One day, shortly after Aug's passing, I was in prayer and received a verse that would become one of my go-to verses. "Have I not commanded you? Be strong and courageous. Do not be afraid; do not be discouraged, for the LORD your God will be with you wherever you go" (Joshua 1:9 NIV). Boy did I ever need to find and learn that verse. It would become my mantra for sure.

It was during this time God showed me he will supply me with enough grace to get through the next 24 hours. "For we live by faith and not by sight" (2 Corinthians 5:7 NIV). That is how I had to look at things. I just had to concentrate on getting through the next 24 hours. I learned that trust, faith, and perseverance were going to be key and I was going to have to walk this path.

I came to realize all the changes I had made years before in finances, faith, and healthy eating were all preparing me for what God knew I would need to endure, for what He knew was going to come in my life and the path I would be walking. I had something I repeated many times to myself off and on throughout the years: "Anxiety and illness do not exist in my body because I am a child of God." I share this because there were times where I walked around the house constantly repeating this to try and keep myself calm. I have found in my experience that grief, depression and anxiety can cause physical illness. I had to find something to counter attack that. I learned anxiety and worry are not the DNA of a believer. I learned not to look too far into the future because that just posed a lot of unneeded anxiety and what-ifs. I learned to live that way, on some days more than others.

One of the hardest things for me to do was to let down my pride and ask for help. It bothered me there were things I could not do on my own and had taken for granted because Aug automatically took care of these things. It infuriated me because here I was, this strong, independent woman, and yet there were things I had no idea how to take care of or do. I'm not the type of person who really wanted to ask for help, but it got to a point on some things when I had no choice. My kids, family, and friends would constantly tell me, "Just ask. That's what we are here for." I had to learn to let my pride and perhaps a little bullheadedness go. It was a humbling experience. There were so many people who wanted to help out. I learned not to be afraid to reach out when I needed a helping hand.

We were busy preparing for my son Brad's wedding in June and my daughter Amanda's wedding in July. As happy and excited as everyone was for the impending nuptials, we all knew they would be very bittersweet as well, since the loss of their dad was so fresh in everyone's mind. I'm happy to report we made it through both of those weddings, which were absolutely beautiful, I might add. Of course, not without a lot of tears, but everyone knew Augie was present and was with us at those special events.

However, as we were preparing for the weddings, my mother's health was continuing to fail. Two weeks before Amanda's wedding, she had a severe stroke. I felt like I was re-living everything I had just been through with Aug. You can imagine the rollercoaster of emotions going on at this point.

Once again, those next days and weeks were filled with hospitals, doctors, tests, rehab and so on. Eventually, she was brought back to her hometown to a nursing home. We unfortunately had to watch our once vibrant mom, grandma, and great-grandma slowly slip away from us. Jean Vosholler lost her battle on August 28, 2016, three days after her 86th birthday. So, on September 1, 2016, seven months after I lost my husband, we laid my mother to rest. When I think back now, I can't believe my body didn't just crumble. However, with my strength of faith, with the resilience and strength of character of my mother, and with the support of family and friends, I once again had to pull up my boot straps and start yet another healing and grieving process.

Healing Takes Time

Grief and the process of grieving has a meaning all of its own. Each person grieves a loss so very differently. I have learned this as I have maneuvered through it with Aug and my mom. There are certain things that will need to be taken care of, and the appropriate time to accomplish those things is an individual decision. Each person takes on this process differently. For me, getting rid of all of Aug's belongings was a process. At one point, I could go through his personal items; another time it was his clothes; another time it was his things in the shed.

Most recently, I was finally ready to get rid of his work boots. They sat in the garage right by the door where he always kept them up until a few months ago. Whenever we had a family cleaning day, the boys would ask if they could get rid of them, and the answer was always no, not yet. I still have yet to let some things go. I still have some things to take care of, but that will be for another time when I'm ready.

On the other hand, my family and I were able to go through my mom's things rather quickly, so it was an entirely different scenario. The one thing I do know is I will never judge someone on how they handle their grief. We are all unique. We all have to do what we have to do to get through the process. Grief never goes away. You just learn to move forward in spite of the grief.

My mother and I always had so many great conversations. I knew she was ready to go be with my dad; however, I was still not ready to let her go. I remember on one occasion shortly after Aug passed we sat at her kitchen table and both cried. I was crying because I had just buried the love of my life and she was crying because she said she wished it would have been her that passed instead of Aug. She said, "He was too young, and it wasn't fair you lost your partner." I said to her in that moment, evidently God still needed her here and her work was not done. Now as I look back on things, once again God's hand was in this. He knew I was going to need my mom to get me through those first months after Aug's passing. He was so right. I can't imagine her going first and then Aug seven months later. I say that because I truly leaned on and depended on my mom. You know a girl always needs her mom, no matter what age you are.

In the midst of all of this, I was trying to continue the work I knew I was put on this earth to do. I had gone to a networking meeting and by chance, met someone who would be invaluable in my grieving and healing process, as well as my personal growth process. It was the first time I had ever went to this actual meeting. Once again, enter divine intervention. I met a woman, Chris. She has helped me in more ways than I can even mention.

When I first started to meet with Chris, she helped me get through the grieving. When you lose two of the most important people in your life in a matter of seven months, there is a huge gaping hole in your heart needing to be healed. As time went on and the healing began, she taught me so many life skills to help me cope. She taught me how to sit with myself and feel the raw emotion going on. She became what I would call a lifeline for me. I can't imagine where I would be without everything she has shared with me. Because of my meetings with her, I have honed in on working to become the best version of me by reading and really digging deep inside to see what it is that I want in life. She continues to mentor me on a regular basis. In fact, she is one of the reasons I decided to write this book.

She would give me what I call homework, and I would actually do the exercises and keep copious notes. I would always report back on my findings, which in turn became great journals of everything I had learned and endured on those following days, weeks, and months. I will share later in more detail some of the many things I have learned from her.

I knew part of my healing was to go back to the hospital where Aug was a patient and to thank them all for everything they had done for him. Believe me when I tell you, I fought this for a few months, because I didn't want to have to do this.

It would have been easy to go back had the outcome been what we had wanted. But to go there, given the outcome we had was an entirely different story. However, I believe in following what God leads me to do. I try to listen and be the best steward I can. I am far from perfect. However, I know if I do what He has called me to do, somehow everything will turn out alright.

On a fateful day in December of 2016, I packed up thank-you care packages for all of the specialty staff that had cared for Aug. I knew this was going to be a day filled with emotion for me, but I also knew God would help me through this as He always had and continues to do. One of the nurses that worked there happened to be my oldest daughter Amanda and her husband Eric's good friend. So with her as my guide and my support, I went to each and every individual department and floor to personally thank them for everything they did.

I cannot tell you how many tears were shed that day, not just by me, but by the many staff members that had remembered us from 10 months earlier. I had no idea how much we had impacted them. However, they remembered us so well, because of how we were there as a family, how we were so loving to Aug, and how we were such a positive force to be around. One of the nurses said she thought of me as a living angel. As we prepared to go to the last department, which was the ICU unit which Aug had been in on his final days, the nurse and I prayed a special prayer as we entered. We both knew that this was going to be especially hard.

As we entered the unit, we walked by the room where Aug had passed. At that very moment, another family was just walking out of the exact room. They too had just lost a loved one. I stopped, frozen in fear and reliving everything they were feeling. They sat with the staff for a few minutes and then exited. I truly wondered if this was even an appropriate time to do this, because loss affects the staff too. However, since I was there, I decided to follow through. After chatting with the staff members, I once again realized God's hand was in this visit.

The staff needed me there at that moment to remember why they do what they do. They of course remembered our family. As we all hugged and cried, it was a moment I will never forget and was so thankful I had followed through on God's nudging. I left the hospital that day emotionally drained but knew it was something I was called to do and felt a peace as I drove home.

There were times where I felt like I couldn't do it. I went through so many different emotions: anger, hatred, hurt, fear, and loneliness. I had this huge fear of what was going to happen next. During this time a certain Bible verse kept appearing in front of me, and I realized I had to stand on that verse. "The LORD has done it this very day; let us rejoice today and be glad" (Psalms 118:24 NIV).

Laying in bed one night, I felt like I was in a cocoon, and there was a crack, and I could see the bright light of my life, but I needed to break that open. I fell on my knees and cried out to the Lord, praying and crying for answers. The next day, I realized the anxiety and fear that I had been feeling was all about control. I couldn't control what had happened to Aug or my mom. All through Aug's illness and doctor appointments my thought was, *I am going to save him*. Once again, I had to realize that God was in control and not me. All of the loss I had suffered made me feel as though I was out of control, and the reason behind the anxiety. The cocoon had been broken for me. It was like a spiritual awakening. I wanted to get my happiness back. I actually found it was easier to be happy than it was to be sad. Sadness is very draining. It sucks you into a pit.

Through my continued self-work, I came to realize it was possible some of my anxiety stemmed back to when I was born. My parents had mentioned the hospital I was born in was under construction. My mom once said jackhammers were going off while we were there. She said every time the jackhammers would start, I would be startled and start crying. You see sometimes things that are going on in your life can stem back to your childhood, or in my case, back to when I was born.

As we approached the one year anniversary, I knew it was going to be a hard day to relive. We had made it through the first year of all the firsts. The day of the anniversary of Aug's death, I sat and wrote how I had grown and was provided for since his passing. As I looked back, I was amazed at everything that had transpired and how I had actually grown from these great losses.

I had started to plan a vacation for February 2017 before Aug had become sick. We were going to celebrate Aug's 60th birthday and our 15th anniversary. I had planned a surprise getaway with all of the kids and grandkids. A few months after his passing, I asked the kids if they wanted to still go. Everyone agreed it would be a good time for a family get-together.

In February 2017, we all took off for a family getaway to beautiful Siesta Key Beach, FL. Looking back now, it probably couldn't have come at a better time. I felt like it was a time of healing for all of us. We had a great time full of laughter and tears. I knew it was what we needed as a family. I have since decided to make this an annual getaway for me. A time to reflect and rejuvenate. For me, there is no place better to do this than by the ocean, palm trees, and sugar-white, sandy beaches. After losing Aug and my mom so close together, I really started to think about my own mortality and what kind of legacy I wanted to leave behind.

After I returned from my trip to Florida and was continuing to heal, another piece of the healing process came from sifting through and jotting down the many things that I loved and missed about Augie and my mom. Here are some of my most fondest memories of both of them.

My mother lived a good, full life. She loved her family. She had tons of friends. She had a smile on her face all the time. She enjoyed herself whatever she was doing. "I have no regrets," she would tell me every time we got together. That was what she was remembered for. What a great legacy.

To know him was to love him. Because Aug was gone far too early as far as I'm concerned, the healing has taken a bit longer. There are so many things that I miss about him like his uncanny ability to make me laugh and his life-of-the-party personality, his hard work ethic. As one of his good friends said, "If Aug was there you could always count on having a good time!" He would say, "You gotta get up every day and milk the cows." He would come up with hilarious one-liners. I love sitting with family and friends as we share Augie stories and what we have now re-named as "Augie-isms."

He'd joke with me that after he was dead, I couldn't holler at him anymore. He would say, "Joycie, I will probably be the only guy who dies and still gets hollered at." Well, I'd like to say that's not true; however, I'm not gonna lie. When there are things that I can't take care of on my own that he always took care of, I am like, "Dang it Aug." Poor guy is still hearing it.

Aug made a huge impact on the community of St Rose. He was born and lived his entire life in St. Rose. He was St Rose proud! It is what he considered God's Country, and he let everyone know it.

Aug was active in the community. He was a volunteer fireman for over 20 years. He was a member of the St. Rose Development Club for over 40 years holding various offices. He was an officer of St. Rose Township. In addition, he was a Knights of Columbus member, a Highland Moose member, an active Mason, and a Shriner.

Aug left a legacy like no other. He touched the lives of so many. It was evident at his funeral visitation and mass. People came by the hundreds to show their respect. The community even commented they had never seen a funeral mass so crowded that extra chairs had to be set up to house everyone. As sad as it was, it definitely makes my heart sing to know he had left such an imprint on so many people!

After Aug's passing, the family decided to hold two fundraisers in his memory. The Putzing-Around Jeep Run in memory of Augie Barth raised over $35,000, which was given back to his four favorite charities—SRDC, Masonic Lodge 583, the Ma-Cli-Bo Shriners, and the St. Rose Fire Department. Hundreds of people attended and donated to these events. Wow, we as a family were blown away. Talk about a lasting legacy.

But what was most important to him was his family. His four children and their significant others and his grandsons were what he lived for. Every one of the kids had a special place as he labeled them. These beautiful kids are the reason I choose to go on every day. Each one of them has amazing and unique qualities.

Amanda was dubbed "the oldest." She is married to Eric and has one son, Jacob. Aug shared with me that as Amanda was born premature, she fought for her life as she was a mere four pounds, and he could hold her in the palm of one hand. She will do anything for anyone, is fiercely protective, and is everyone's second mom. She is an amazing wife to Eric and is an awesome mom to Jacob, who truly remembers his papa Augie and tells me how he misses him but still sees him by the moon.

Brad was referred to as "my boy." He is married to Kirsten and has two sons, Maverick August (Augs namesake) and Dawsen, whom Aug never got to meet. Brad is the man he is today because of Aug giving him responsibility at a young age and trusting him as a child on the farm. He's grown to be an exceptional man who is a loving husband and devoted father to his boys.

Megan was "the favorite" simply because she was the middle child and Aug felt she needed a special place too. She is the child who wants to make sure everyone is happy and does everything she can to please everyone. She is the softy of the family with her huge heart and is a fabulous wife to Alan.

Kayla was "the youngest." She is the energizer bunny reincarnated. This girl has a zest for life and fun, and she never stops. Aug always said she never knew a stranger because even as a small child she would go up to a stranger and say,

"Hello friend." She and her significant other Brad make a great team and couple.

Aug was so glad to see each of the children had found a life partner that made them happy. We chatted so many times in those last months about what an amazing and great family we had. I know without a doubt, Aug is everyone's guardian angel and is smiling down on all of them as they continue on life's journey.

Joyce Barth

Looking for Signs

As time went on, I was constantly looking for signs of Aug and my mom. There are always signs all around us like the penny on the ground, the feather flowing through the air, the butterfly appearing, or the gorgeous red Cardinal. I constantly prayed for Aug and my mom to come to me in a dream to let me know that they were okay. I have yet to have those dreams. I am okay with that. They may not be with me physically, but they are always in my heart and their spirit lives on. This has taken me time to learn to process, but it definitely helps with my positive attitude.

I have also had a couple of what I will call non-traditional signs. A smashed up Busch Light can and a random blog that I came upon late one Sunday night were such non-traditional signs. A year or so after Aug's passing, I had collected many pennies, saw the butterflies, collected a few feathers, and had a couple of cardinals appear. I was questioning the timing of removing my wedding rings. Having never been a widow before, my question was, "How do you know when it's time to take off your rings?" Unfortunately there isn't a guide book answering all of these questions.

I went searching Google for the answer. My motto has always been, "Google has the answer for everything." I typed in my search and wow, every person on the planet (or so it seemed) had the answer to my question. I started clicking on a few blogs, and all of a sudden I clicked on one that totally caught my attention and knew immediately it was the one I needed to read. It was to be my answer. I knew this was my article, because the person sharing the blog just happened to be in the same line of direct sales work that I was in.

She shared her story of how she lost her husband and the next year went on to excel in her sales business and had won a diamond ring from the company. She replaced her wedding ring with that company ring and felt as though it was the perfect tribute to her late husband. This

struck me simply because at that very moment I
was also working on the exact goal that she had
just shared in the blog. I knew this was a nudging
from the Lord. So I spent the next three months
working on that exact goal. I felt that if this was
to be my transition, then if I worked, God would
provide. Once again He came through for me. I
met my goal and earned the company ring.
Believe me, there were many emotions that went
along with this accomplishment, happy emotions
and tearful emotions. I can proudly say that when
I went across the stage to pick up my ring in a
beautiful sequin, blingy gown just as I imagined I
would wear as a young girl, I blew three kisses up
to heaven. One to God, one to Aug, and one to
my mom. The moment when I picked up the
ring, I knew it was time to transition and okay to
remove my wedding rings.

The smashed-up Busch Light can was a whole
other story. I had been praying for answers about
something at the car wash I owned. Of course,
the car wash was Aug's baby and desire to own.
There had been many times since he passed, I

would be at the car wash trying to get things taken care of and would be hollering at him. On this specific Monday morning, he was getting one of those talks. I said, "Dang it Aug I sure wish you would give me an answer!" He sure did.

Earlier that morning, I had picked up all of the trash laying around the car wash. The last place I had picked up the trash was in front of the soda machine, right before I checked what flavors needed to be refilled. I did my normal Monday soda run. When I returned 30 minutes later, I was parking, and I noticed something laying right by the soda machine (I had just picked up the trash 30 minutes earlier). I remember thinking, *What the heck is that laying there?* As I walked up to it, I realized it was a smashed up can. I jokingly thought, *if it's a Busch Light can smashed up there is my answer from Aug.* As I approached the can to pick it up, sure enough, it was a Busch Light can smashed up. I just had to laugh because that can represented an answer I needed. Busch Light was Aug's beverage of choice. The can being in that particular spot at that particular moment definitely was a sign. If you are looking for signs, make sure you keep yourself aware. You just never know in what form they might come. I still laugh to this day about that sign. Gotta love my Augie!

Joyce Barth

Self-Care a Must

As I was healing from the losses, I decided I wanted to work on being the best version of me I could be. I want to share with you what I focus on daily to make that happen. That is my main goal in life. I want to bless others and bring them joy. I want to be the best steward I can be, so that everything I do will glorify God. That is my daily prayer.

Pursuing this takes work. It takes daily discipline, and it takes a willingness to want to better one self. I have always wanted to have a platform to share my beliefs, to share my outlook, to share what I've learned and to give hope to others. I always thought it would be through my direct sales business. It has given me a platform to share these things. However, since the death of my husband and mother, I honestly think my platform has stretched to a larger arena across the board. I had no idea I would be able to touch so many lives, but I constantly receive messages from people on what an inspiration I am, asking me how I have continued on in life given so much loss in such a short amount of time.

Everything starts with daily discipline. When you take God as your partner and grab on to His hand, He will lead you and get you through anything life throws at you. I'm a living testament to that. I'm so thankful for that. I can't imagine how my life might have turned out otherwise.

I am a huge proponent of prayer time first thing in the morning. It gets me grounded for the day. I find my day goes much smoother when I take this time daily. I have fallen in love with journaling. I wasn't always this way. However, through the years, it has been such an instrument of healing for me. In the morning, I journal my prayers, my thoughts, whatever is on my mind. I ask the Lord what lessons he wants me to learn through all of this.

Looking back now, I know He wanted me to learn to lean on and rely on Him. He wanted me to learn to have faith and believe He would get me through this. Many of my prayers asked for peace-comfort-strength-wisdom-courage-discernment-and grace. Sometimes I would specifically ask for super-strength. I would also speak positive words of encouragement and hope. I want to be a beacon of hope to inspire and encourage others.

In the evening, I take time to do a gratitude journal. I find three to five things every day I am thankful for. Now there have been times where that always has not been easy, especially in the midst of certain circumstances. However, there is always something to be thankful for no matter what. By doing this, it has really helped me through the tough times. It gives me perspective from the day and helps me rest better. Even in those days when Aug was fighting for his life, I made sure to continue this practice as I needed it more than I could have ever realized. I continue to do this and also have incorporated a brief review of the day's activities simply because I want to remember each day and whose paths I crossed. It's a joyful feeling for me.

I also do what I call a brain dump. That is just a written list of everything that was and is going on in my brain. It can be absolutely anything. Just basically everything that is bothering me or bugging me. It really helps once I have written it down. It somehow alleviates my stress and helps me to declutter my brain. It is interesting to go back after a bit of time has passed to see how many of those things on that dump list were taken care of.

I always ask myself what I am feeding my mind. I don't watch much television or read the paper or listen to the news. I've always been taught leaders are readers. I had to teach myself to even like to read a book. But over time, I have found I have grown to enjoy reading books. Especially those which help me to become a better version of myself. If you aren't a reader, you can always listen to audio books. Some people are just better listeners and get more from a book. I shared earlier with you about the one book that was instrumental in my weight loss. The other book that has been instrumental in my overall thinking is *Shift for Good,* also written by Tory Johnson. To me, school is never out for the pro. It's important to continue to grow myself as a person.

I also plug into podcasts. *Ted Talks*, *Brene Brown*, and *Oprah Super Soul Sunday* are some of my faves. I also have a few favorite pastors that I plug into as well, Steven Furtick, Joyce Meyer, and Joel Osteen are a few that really speak to me.

I encourage you to find good mentors to bounce ideas off of. I have been blessed to have found people in different areas of my life. You have those people too in your life. Pray for them to be revealed and then follow the Holy Spirit's promptings to reach out to them. It may be scary, but that's ok, reach out anyway. You will be so glad that you did. To become the best version of you, we sometimes have to do things that make us uncomfortable at first, but the payoff will be so great and life altering!

For me, I look at the people that are in my life, and I ask myself if they add value or if they sometimes drain me. Obviously there are some people that are in our lives that can do both at the same time. We don't have choices of who some of those people are, however, sometimes we do have a choice with whom we spend our time with and how much time we spend with those people.

I pray people in and out of my life. Sounds harsh? Not at all. My main goal is to touch lives. I ask God constantly to bring those people into my path whose life I can touch in one way or another. Or perhaps they can touch and change my life as well. It's a constant two-way street. I also ask if there are people in my life who are no longer supposed to be in my path, for God to move them out of it. It is not a bad thing at all, only because people outgrow each other. Sometimes values don't line up. Other times, the relationship was meant for a season or a reason. We all have people who come and go from our lives. It's just part of who we are.

I believe one of the best things a person can do is to become others-focused. I knew I was going to have to stay active. I'm active with both of my businesses. I stay active in my community to be involved and give back there. I'm active to make sure I continue to cultivate the relationships that are important to me. A good friend of mine once told me that as you grow older, things become less important and relationships with family and friends become key. At that time, which was about 15 plus years ago, relationships were important, but having nice things was equally important. So I wasn't quite grasping that. But oh, how I now know exactly what she was talking about. A day of shopping doesn't give me an ounce of the joy I feel after a day of spending time with family or friends or meeting with clients or someone who needs to see a smiling face. I tell people all the time that relationships are the most important to me these days. It is relationships that I value most.

I've changed my expectation level. I know that I am enough. I had let past hurts define me and give me an I-am-not-enough mentality. I had to work through that and change that thought process. Again, it took willingness to be vulnerable and do the self-care work I needed to do to get to this point in my life. I expect great things to happen in all areas of my life. I have seven areas that I personally focus on regularly: spiritual, financial, emotional, healthy eating, exercise, business, and personal growth.

About a year ago, I was diagnosed with a small heart murmur, nothing serious; however, the doctor has strongly encouraged me to incorporate regular exercise into my daily routine. I'm still working on that one, but I am confident I will get this one figured out too. I am a pretty determined person.

Moving Forward – God Winks

These last couple of years have been the hardest of my life. I am also at a total peaceful place in my life. Sometimes God sneaks our strength in through sorrow. I can't really explain it, but in the midst of the loss, I have found strength, courage, wisdom, resilience, and grace that I didn't know I had. There have been times where I've just had to totally surrender it all because I didn't know what else to do. However, I cannot put a price tag on the joy I exude and feel. I thank God every day for all of the hundreds of blessings that He bestows on me. I have a beautiful canvas hanging in my room I received as a gift. It is the first thing I see every morning when I awake. It simply reads *Today I Choose Joy*. That is how I choose to start my day. I encourage you to find a positive quote that speaks to you and place it somewhere that you see it first thing in the morning. It really will set your tone for the day before your feet hit the ground running.

What do I do when I don't know what to do?
I pray and ask for guidance. For me it has been
the one thing that has answered anything I needed
in my life. I've had many "God winks"
throughout the years, and my friends, I believe if
you sit back and think about it, you probably have
too.

I had always been an avid music buff. I love all
genres of music because it has always brought me
to a happy place in my spirit. After Aug passed, I
almost felt guilty listening to music. For the
longest time, I never wanted to turn the stereo
on in my house or listen to music in the car.

Ironically, one day I had lunch with a
girlfriend. She told me about a song I should
listen to. I started crying and told her about not
wanting to listen to music anymore. She made
me promise to go home and listen to the song at
least. I did, and it immediately started to give me
some healing. A few days later, another girlfriend
of mine stopped by my house. She had been
listening to the radio and heard three songs in a
row that she felt were Aug speaking to me

through her via this music. Once again, I was receptive. I took the time to listen to the songs she shared with me. I shed many, many tears listening to these songs. It did continue to heal my heart and soul. Today, I am back to being my music-listening, music-loving self, singing along to all my favorite tunes. Isn't it amazing how God uses people to pass on a message?

I strive to try and hear what the Holy Spirit leads me to do. Sometimes I miss it, but when something or someone is put in my path, I feel it is happening for a reason, and I pray about the situation or person. It may seem bigger than you. It may not make any sense in the flesh or in human concept, yet you know to follow through on something. This exact situation happened to me a year and a half after Aug passed away. I reconnected with an old friend that I hadn't seen for a few years. We had a connection that couldn't be explained. I prayed for guidance with this person because they were in a very bad place in their life. God spoke to me to be a source of light and guidance and hope to this individual. He

95

told me that it may not be easy but I must stay the course. As I prayed about this person regularly, the conviction became stronger and more specifics were revealed to me. There were struggles for sure, and it was not an easy road for me to take as I was met with a lot of opposition. However, I knew this was not about me but about how I could be a blessing in someone's life. So I stayed the course, and in that year the reason I was given as to why and how I was to be in this person's life came to light and the healing process for this friend has begun. Praise God for that! I am soooo glad that I listened and was obedient to do what God put before me, even though it made zero sense to me in the flesh. I share this story with you because many times we want to quickly dismiss people or things that come into our path, however, there is usually a reason for it, and in this case I was meant to be there to help this person through a very dark time in their life.

The Lord also gave me another recent opportunity to be a blessing to a friend in need. I didn't know there was a need, but after some conversations, I realized that I could somehow help them out and take away some stress for them. It was a great feeling for me to be a blessing. This person asked me why I did what I did and my response to them was this, "I remember a time when I was in need, and someone was there to help me out. I've never forgotten that person, and I vowed that someday I would pay it forward, so I am doing just that." I know without a doubt we will forever have a special bond because of this, and they were so appreciative. I went on to say to this friend, "I know you will remember this moment, and someday when you are in a position to, I just ask that you pay it forward as well." I'm not telling you all of this to say look how great I am but rather to impart on how important it is to be there for others. I was humbled that He gave me the opportunity to do this.

As I shared with you the writing of this book has been healing and therapeutic for me. I want to share in detail just how God-ordained this book has been. I've never had the desire to write a book. In fact, if you remember, I said I wasn't always the best reader, so to write a book was beyond anything I ever considered. However, God's hand has truly been in the writing of this. As this started to unfold, I had a couple of random friends make mention that I should write a book. Well, I laughed them off and told them, "No, that's not going to happen." I won't tell you what I truly said to them.

When my therapist Chris and I had talked about it a few different times, I was still not sure. However, in September of 2017 when I was heading to California to visit my friend Kelly and her husband Mike, Chris asked me to open myself to the possibility and to really soul-search while I was gone. I always want to make sure I keep an open mind, so I made the promise that while I was there, I would be prayerful about the opportunity. One morning while I was sitting with Kelly and Mike at breakfast, Kelly and I were chatting about life, and her husband Mike looked to me and asked me, "Have you ever considered writing a book? You have such a story to share."

Well I must admit I was taken back by this because the mention of a book never came up while we were chatting, not to mention, that I had only met Kelly's husband two times previously. So to have him suggest this truly caught my attention. As the trip unfolded, the last morning I was there, all of these words started coming to me, which in turn became the first pages of the book. Then the title of the book also was given to me. I'm like, "Wowsa, if that's not a sign I don't know what is." Funny thing is, I went to California with just my luggage and my phone. I had nothing to write with or write on. I immediately grabbed my phone and started placing this info there, because I knew all of this was something I better get into print because I surely wouldn't remember it all by the time I got home.

As the story continues, I am writing away, off-and-on, and it's Spring of 2018. The fear of what's next set in. I'd never written a book, and I had no idea how to edit it or publish it. These thoughts ran through my mind for weeks.

On a Wednesday morning in April, I was sitting in my prayer chair and asking God to put someone in my path that could help me figure this all out if this book is truly meant to be. As it might happen, I had lunch plans with a good girlfriend, Julie. I was kind of in a funk that day and wasn't even excited about lunch; however, I hadn't seen her for so long and really wanted to catch up with what was going on in her life.

So we met and as we sat down, she said that she had two things she wanted to chat with me about after we were done with lunch and catching up. So once we got done with lunch and were pretty much caught up, I said, "Okay, what do you want to talk with me about." She said, "Well you probably will tell me no on both of these, but I still want to ask you." I said, "Okay, go on, ask away." Julie asked me her first question, and I immediately answered, "No." I went on and said, "Okay, next question?" She kind of giggled, and said, "Okay well you will

probably tell me no on this as well, but have you
ever considered writing a book?" Well when she
asked me this, I got a big smile on my face, and
said, "Well now that you mention it, I have been
working on something, however," and before I
could even finish my sentence, she told me if I
needed any help with the book, that she had
contacts and resources that could help me
through the process. Needless to say, I started to
cry at this point, because it was that very morning
I had prayed for God to put someone in my path
who could help me with the next steps.

By the time I shared all of this with her, we
were both crying, but oh what a huge God wink
for sure. As she and I talked that day about the
book, a gal walked into the restaurant who had
just lost her husband a few months before. As I
sat and hugged this gal and chatted with her I
tried to give her hope for her future. As she
walked away, Julie looked at me and said, "This is
exactly why you need to finish writing this book.
It is to help people just like that who are going

through what you've gone through." I would have to agree with her.

As the story continued to unfold, I woke up one morning and felt compelled to contact a gal whose name was put on my heart to see if she knew any publishers. This gal is an entrepreneur, so I felt she may have a contact or two. Of course she did, so I contacted a friend of hers, and shared my story with her, not knowing if my sort of story would even have any interest to readers. She explained to me that my sort of story is just what people are wanting to read these days— stories of inspiration, healing, hope, and self-help.

Again, I felt like another answer for me to continue the process of completing this book. I told her that I felt stuck at the moment, and she said just to continue asking myself, "What happened next?" and that would help unblock where I was stuck at. The other thing she shared with me was that the ending was important and that I could work back from there. So again, I'm like, "How am I going to end the book?" Well one afternoon I was sitting at my table eating lunch, and the last sentences were very vividly given to me. I ran to the computer before I would forget what I felt was given, typed those words in, and worked backward from there. Oh Thank You Lord for all of this.

Please believe me when I say this book has been a divine intervention. My continual daily prayer as I finished the book up was, "Lord, please give me all of the words that need to be in this book that will bless others, and remove those that don't need to be in the book." As I've said to all my family and friends, if this book touches one person's life, then it's done its job, as I truly want it to be a blessing to those who read it. And with that being said, it's been healing for me so I know it's touched and changed my life as well.

Looking back, it amazes me and moves me to tears when I think back about how God's hand has been in every part of my life. It didn't always make sense, but the saying is when God closes a door, he opens a window. "'For I know the plans I have for you,' declares the LORD, 'plans to prosper you and not to harm you, plans to give you hope and a future'" (Jeremiah 29:11 NIV). God already knows what's going to happen in our lives and has a plan, so there is no sense in worrying about how this or that is going to turn out.

Family and Friends are Everything

Since you all know I love to share stories, here is a funny story for you. A few girlfriends and I are at a Cardinal Baseball game, and the section we are sitting in happens to have a lot of people that I know. As people would pass by, they would say hi, and of course I said hi back. Well, after a couple of hours this going on, a young couple sitting behind us tapped me on the shoulder and said, "Hey are you somebody important?" I giggled and said, "No, why on earth would you ask that?" The kids reply was "Well heck, everyone around her knows you so we thought you had to be somebody important!" He said I reminded him of Norm from the show *Cheers!* I totally cracked up at that response, but after he made that comment, it did make me take stock of just how lucky I am to have so many friends.

God has blessed me with so much and has protection over me. "Jabez cried out to the God of Israel, 'Oh, that you would bless me and enlarge my territory! Let your hand be with me, and keep me from harm so that I will be free from pain.' And God granted his request" (1 Chronicles 4:10 NIV). I could go on and on. The life I get to live on a daily basis, the great health He has blessed me with.

Let's talk about family and family of choice for a moment. Everyone has people in their life whether they are blood relatives or friends or co-workers in one's life who are always there when we need them. Those people that we can count on in trying times. I've been abundantly blessed with a lot of special people who have each played a significant part in my life and healing process.

Meeting and marrying Aug has blessed me with an amazing family. The four kids, their significant others, and the grandsons are the highlight of my life and the reason that I continue to move forward every day and be the best version of me that I can be for them. I may not get to see them all of the time because of crazy-busy life schedules, but believe me when I say they are always in my heart and I think of them constantly. I cannot imagine my life without any of them.

The Vosholler family is made up of my siblings, sisters-in-law, nieces, nephews, great nieces, and great nephews; they have truly been by my side for everything in my life. I've always been able to count on them no matter what was going on. When Aug and the kids came into my life, my family truly embraced them all and have had soooo much fun over the years. Lots of fun memories and laughs for sure. I'm blessed beyond measure with the family I was born into. It may get loud and crazy at our family functions, but I would not have it any other way.

The Barth family welcomed me with open arms when Aug and I got together. I'm not quite sure they knew what to think about me, but they have been such a source of strength for me and continue to include me as family. We've had some pretty amazing and memorable family get-togethers, some lasting into the wee hours of the morning when Euchre playing was involved or the boys decided it was time to have more cocktails. I truly could not have married into a better family and am proud to be part of this family.

In addition to the kids, my family, and Aug's family who are always there no matter what I need, we have a huge extended family as well that is always there. I am also blessed to have what I call "family of choice." These are people that are in my life, and although not officially family, they have become family to myself and the kids over the years.

First I have the St. Rose go-to family. This group of people have been family to Aug and the kids forever. Even though I've known many of them for years, when I came into Aug's life, they truly embraced me as family as well. I'm so very blessed to have them in my life. They have been such a source of support to all of us and are there no matter what is needed. Couldn't have a better group than this in my corner!

I also have Aug's adopted family, the Meyer Clan. They've always loved Aug and the kids, and I've been friends with these peeps forever, and we've shared lots of good times and sad times with each other. All of them always are there and stick by the kids and I. They joke that Aug was their redheaded step-brother and that I am the angel that came into his and the kids life. I feel so blessed to be part of their clan!

I can't forget our Shriner family for sure. When Aug joined the Ma-Cli-Bo Shriners, we became so close and spent so much time with these people that they did become family to us. They have been such a source of support, and we've also had a lot of fun together. I can't imagine what my life would be like if they weren't in it!

My MK family has been with me for 25 years. Lordy, these gals have been through the good, the bad, and the ugly with me. We've laughed, cried, prayed, traveled, shopped together, and have so many memories to share. They are always there for whatever is needed and know that the kids and I can always count on them.

And then there are my lifetime friends and school friends. Golly, they have been in my life longer than I can remember. Let's just say we span decades of memories. Some of us go back as far as grade school, but I know for sure that no matter what has gone on through the years, these folks have supported me through my ups and downs, and I truly am blessed to have each of them as family.

The newest group that has come into my life is what I will dub as my Jeep Family, also known as my Jeeples. I have met sooooo many great people in the past couple of years while out jeep riding and doing the charity runs, and truly these people have become like family to me! Some of these people I've known for years and others I've just met, but they have truly embraced me and I them. As I've always said, "You can never have too many friends in life." This is a group that I also know I can count on for support.

His hand, my journey

There have literally been hundreds of people that have been there as I've gone through the healing process these last three years. Whether they have been there by my side in person, sent me a note, or prayed for me, please know that I have not forgotten any person and hold each close to my heart.

Joyce Barth

A New Normal

As our lives continue to find some normalcy, I settled into some day-to-day routines. My direct sales business continued to flourish, and the carwash became my second business. Both continued to keep me very busy. Most recently, I decided I needed to make some changes and sold the carwash in the beginning of 2019 to allow myself to focus on other projects and opportunities.

In the spring of 2017, our small community officially became an incorporated village. I became the first female trustee for the Village of St. Rose. I took on this position for a lot of reasons; namely, because Aug was such a huge proponent of our community incorporating that I had no doubt, he would have held a seat on the board for sure. The second reason was that after being approached four different times to run for this position, I evidently had what it took. The third reason was to have the Barth family name in the history books as being on the first ever village board. Another legacy piece to leave.

One of my more recent Facebook posts went like this: "You have to choose to believe in something or you will fall for anything. I choose to believe I can make a difference in someone's life. I can have a positive impact. I choose to have faith I can get through any of life's curve balls that are thrown at me. I choose to believe that life is what we make of it. I've got a lot of life to live yet. I choose to think positive. I choose to have joy in the journey. Seize the moment. Live life out loud. Laugh and have fun. Life is not a dress rehearsal. Once the day is gone, you never get that day back again." You know social media hashtags are the hot thing, and so my hashtags were #myjoymyjourney, #seizethemoment, #blessedtobeablessing, #1luckygal, and most recently, #liveoutloud.

Megan and Alan had gotten married and had a beautiful wedding in November, 2017. Since I didn't have any kids getting married and decided that the house update could be put on hold for another year, I declared 2018 was going to be a year of travel.

Among those were two annual conferences that I always attend and, of course, my annual February rejuvenation trip to Siesta Key, FL. I added a few special destinations in as well. What better way to heal than spending time away with those close to our heart.

My sister turned 60, so I planned a surprise get-away for her in Sunny Key West, FL. We were going to live out a bucket list item for my sister. We embarked on four days of fun and created such great memories. Second row seats at the Little River Band concert may have been the highlight. I do believe it was a trip of a lifetime for her, and I was so glad to be able to surprise her.

I also took a few days to visit my mentor in Wilmington, NC. I absolutely love being in Karlee's space. She is more than a mentor to me. She was there for me when I went through all the dark times in my life spanning back to the last 25 years, so it was so enjoyable to just sit, visit, and catch up with her, her husband, and family.

My grade school friend Tami and I went on our own version of a Thelma and Louise road trip to Texas, Louisiana, and Tennessee. We have been best friends since first grade and had never taken a road trip vacation together. Knowing how life can change in an instant, we decided that it was a trip that couldn't be put off any longer, and it was an adventure.

This last year has taught me about being more spontaneous and not being on such a tight and rigid schedule. I would never suggest to shirk your responsibilities. However, I also realized how much fun could be had when a random friend would call to go boating, hang out at the pool, take an afternoon country cruise, or go do an unplanned lunch. For myself, I know I love to travel and gallivant the countryside whether it be via my yellow Jeep, jetsetting on a plane, or in an automobile doing a road trip. I love to be on the go.

A day of jeeping does not get any better than this: sun beating on my face, wind in my hair, enjoying the beauty of nature all around me with great friends, and, of course, with a few pit stops for a cold Michelob Ultra or two. Yet there are times I enjoy sitting and relaxing in my house or out on my patio enjoying nature with my variety of favorite tunes blasting with me and my best karaoke voice. It's just who I BE.

I want to leave a legacy that I always had a smile on my face, that I touched and inspired people, that I could brighten their day. I want people to feel better about themselves when they leave my space and to feel that I brought joy into their life, that I somehow blessed them in a positive way. I want to be remembered as being a strong, courageous, bold, resilient, independent, vivacious, alive, and enthusiastic person. But above all, I want to make sure when I arrive at the pearly gates, I am greeted with a, "Well done my good and faithful servant." Then I have truly lived my life out the way it was intended to be.

Last fall, St. Rose celebrated their 150th

anniversary celebration. It was an amazing three-day event filled with food, fun, family, friends, and great memories. The weekend ended with a huge parade and fireworks. Aug was so looking forward to this event as the planning had already begun before his illness and passing. The family and I wanted to represent his memory the best way possible in the parade, and we remain forever #barthstrong. I know he is smiling down on us for sure.

It's been three years since Aug passed and two and a half years since my mom passed. For me, I am growing stronger every day. Yes, I still have my moments of grief, that will never go away. However, I have learned to move forward, and those moments of grief aren't as frequent, and they don't last near as long. I recently came across a post that truly spoke to me. It simply stated, "Everything happens for a reason and that reason causes change. Sometimes it hurts. Sometimes it's hard. But in the end its all for God's Best. Never stop trusting what His plans are." While all of this is a hard pill to swallow, I have to have faith that God still has a plan for my life.

As word leaked out about the writing and publishing of this book, a dear friend of mine asked me what made me decide to write the book and to then go on to publish it. I shared that I started to write the book as healing for myself. I continued to write the book as I felt compelled by God that I had a story to tell and share. He understood all of that, but went on to ask, "By publishing it, aren't you pretty much laying yourself and your life out to everyone? And how did you decide that you were okay with doing that?" My answer was, "Yes, it's very scary to put yourself out there for everyone to read about the ups and downs through your life. However, I truly feel that this book can help, give hope, and inspire others. Because of my faith, it's more important for me to take myself out of the picture. I feel that this book has been divinely appointed."

My hope and prayer is that after you've finished reading this book, it has inspired you in some way, whether you have a test you need to pass or a mountain you keep going around. If you are grieving, I pray this book has given you hope and strength to carry on. I sincerely hope it has somehow impacted your life. Perhaps you are looking to become a better version of you. I'd like to think this book has shed some light on all of these areas. We are all a continual work in progress on this journey called life.

What does the next chapter in my book of life look like? I'm not sure, but I know God has a plan for it, and I'm ready for that ride! Hang on, it's gonna be FUN I'm sure!

Carpe Diem!

Epilogue

I believe we've all been given many gifts, and it's up to us as to how we use those gifts that are so important in our day to day lives. I've worn a lot of hats and been dubbed a lot of names these past years. Party Joycie, Bright Lights Big City Joycie, Hoytie Toytie Joycie, Joycie the fish fry boss lady, but Joycie the author was not one I had ever considered! Did I ever think I would be the person to write a book? Absolutely not, and it was NEVER on my radar to do something like this. However, I have been told many times that I am gifted with my words and how I share things. When people told me I give off positive energy and glow, I knew that was truly a gift from the Lord. I've always prayed I could emit the light of Jesus through myself, touch lives, and bless people to glorify God. I felt this book would be a way to do that. For me, it took a trip to California just to have some down time. Writing this book has continued my healing process. It has been very therapeutic for me.

Acknowledgements

I'm dedicating this book to my late husband, Augie, who I miss so much, but who truly gave me the life I have today. The almost 17 years we spent together shaped and molded me. We had our ups and downs, but I would not have had it any other way. We had FUN and lived our life out loud. I love and miss you, AB!

To my amazing mother, Jean, whom I lost seven months after Aug. You were my best friend, my guidance counselor, my shopping partner, and so much more. You taught me strength and resilience like no other. You left a legacy for sure, and I only hope I can continue to make you and Dad proud as I go through the rest of my life. I know the two of you are dancing up a storm in heaven.

To my beautiful kids and grandsons: Amanda, Eric, and Jacob Detmer; Brad, Kirsten, Maverick, and Dawsen Barth; Megan and Alan Winkeler; and Kayla Barth and Brad Budde. I am honored and blessed to be your mom and granny/grandma. You are the reason I truly get up every day. I LOVE you all so much and am forever grateful that we are family.

To my siblings Ron, Dave, and Joan, to Aug's siblings, Mary and Ben, and all of my in-laws (or outlaws as we affectionately call them), nieces and nephews, great nieces and great nephews, thank you for all of your love and support you show me. I don't know what I would do without any of you.

To my spiritual mentors Karlee, Connie, and Terry. You have given me a piece in my life that I didn't know was missing. I hope to have the forever glow that you all have.

To the amazing Chris. You came into my life by chance meeting. You have guided me, mentored me, encouraged me, and reminded me to be all that I can be and to continue to work on becoming the best version of myself. Thank you for nudging me to keep great journals. To actually follow my heart.

To Kelly and Mike, thank you for welcoming me into your home that random weekend in September.

To Julie, you had connections to help me through the process.

And lastly and most importantly to God and Jesus, His son. I promised to give you all the Praise, Honor, and Glory. My main goal in life is to be a good servant to You and to bless others in the process. I do hope I am doing just that. Thank you for allowing me to be the King's kid and to have that royal blood running through my veins.

About the Author

Joyce (Vosholler) Barth was born in July 1964 and was raised in Highland, IL. Her parents were Fred and Jean, and she has three siblings: Ron, Dave, and Joan. She attended Highland High School, and upon graduation went to work in St. Louis, MO for Lawton-Byrne-Bruner Insurance Agency, and then on to General American Life Insurance Company. In September 1993, she went to work for The Wallstreet Journal and also started her career with Mary Kay Cosmetics, an international skin care and cosmetics company. She left the Wallstreet Journal in May of 1995 to pursue her career with Mary Kay full-time. In October 1999 she moved to St. Rose, IL. In March of 2002 she married Augie Barth and became a "mom" to Amanda, Brad, Megan, and Kayla. She has three grandsons: Jacob, Maverick, and Dawsen. She keeps herself very active in the community as a Village Trustee and St. Rose Development Club member. For her, faith, family, and friends are everything. She enjoys traveling, jeeping, listening to music, and sitting out on her patio enjoying everything life has to offer. She just celebrated her 25th anniversary with Mary Kay Cosmetics in a management position as an Independent Sales Director.

Made in the USA
Columbia, SC
10 August 2019